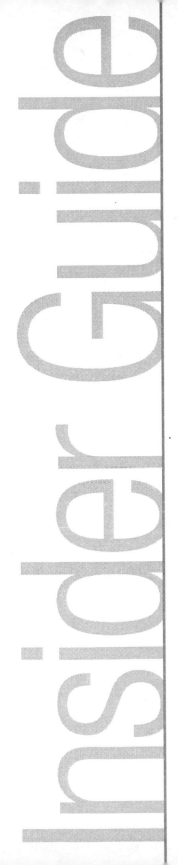

Killer Cover Letters and Resumes! The WetFeet Insider Guide

2004 Edition

Helping you make smarter career decisions.

WetFeet Inc.

609 Mission Street
Suite 400
San Francisco, CA 94105

Phone: (415) 284-7900 or 1-800-926-4JOB
Fax: (415) 284-7910
E-mail: info@wetfeet.com
Website: www.wetfeet.com

Killer Cover Letters and Resumes! The WetFeet Insider Guide

By Rosanne Lurie
ISBN: 1-58207-371-6

Table of Contents

Putting Your Best Foot Forward

- Overview

- The Bottom Line

Overview

Most job hunters today tend to view the search for work as casting a net and hoping that an opportunity is ensnared. Certainly an approach like this can bring results, but a lot of effort is wasted as well. Honing the instruments you use to capture the interest of employers will take the mystery, and some of the frustration, out of the process. You need to understand what employers look for in the initial review of applications, and what qualities will lead you to the next stage in the hiring process. The ease of posting jobs online means more people will apply for the same position, while changes in the economy and job market mean that today's employers can afford to be extra choosy. Now, more than ever, you need to find ways to put yourself ahead of the pack.

To get some sense of the employers' perspective, check out this bit of information: Recently, ResumeDoctor.com contacted more than 5,000 recruiters and hiring managers throughout the United States and Canada regarding the success of using online job postings. More than 92 percent of those surveyed reported being inundated with irrelevant responses to their job postings. Most participants indicated that they receive hundreds of responses per online job posting.

Additional complaints included:

- A majority of resumes do not match the job description. [71%]
- Job seekers "blasting out" unsolicited resumes. [63%]
- Job seekers fail to follow specific resume submission instructions found in job post. [34%]

Mike Worthington of ResumeDoctor.com says, "Most online job postings bury recruiters with literally hundreds of resumes. . . . The ease that job seekers can respond to postings online is now their greatest obstacle."

For more information, visit www.ResumeDoctor.com or see the resource section at the end of this guide.

One of the best ways to impress employers is to avoid these all-too-common errors. Whether you're just out of college, changing careers, or a seasoned professional looking to make the next career move, this guide will help you do the best possible job of presenting your qualifications to recruiters and hiring managers in the United States. Although "perfect" application materials won't necessarily land you a job—there's a lot more to getting a job offer than sending a good resume—this guide will give you valuable insight into what employers are seeking, and how to develop materials that reflect your strengths.

For starters, you'll learn about the best ways to prepare for your job search, including how to determine and articulate your strengths, research techniques, and how to customize your presentation towards desired positions and organizations. Next, you'll get the full scoop on how to create a killer resume and cover letter— from what information it should (and shouldn't) contain to how it should look and sound. Multiple cover letter and resume examples, as well as suggestions for creating layouts that suit your unique needs, will give you great ideas for how your own materials should look and sound. The section on special concerns examines common problem areas—such as international careers, "overqualified" candidate syndrome, or long time gaps—with helpful suggestions for how to address them. The final section contains suggestions for following up your application, as well as resources that will help you in your job search.

The Bottom Line

At best, resume readers spend 30 seconds reviewing a cover letter or resume the first time. This is especially true in a competitive job market, where recruiters receive up to 200 responses to advertised job postings. In 30 seconds, an excellent cover letter and resume package needs to convey an image of who you are, what you're capable of, and how you have used your abilities to accomplish results. Ideally, it indicates that you know yourself well and have a firm grasp on what you bring to the table. In a nutshell, your cover letter and resume are less about where you have been than about where you want to go next.

Although insiders tell us "there isn't one right answer" to the question of how to create a good cover letter or resume (phew!), they say the best materials are concise, results-oriented, and very clearly presented. Of course, a great resume alone won't land you the job of your dreams, but appropriate choices in shaping your materials make you far more likely to get a call, and can even help you sail more smoothly through the interview process. This guide will show you the way.

Are you ready to begin? Let's dive in!

On Your Mark, Get Set, Prep!

- Doing Your Due Diligence

- Three Steps for Effective Research

- Where to Look

- Why Research?

- "Bottom Line" Skills

- Determining What You Have to Offer

- Analyzing Your Transferable Skills

- Exercises

Doing Your Due Diligence

You may come to the job search armed with a great track record at work and school, numerous promotions and awards, and affiliations with prestigious institutions that most only dream of visiting. Or maybe this doesn't describe you at all, and you worry about how you will ever measure up. Whatever your background, you can be sure that you will not progress far in the job market without doing your due diligence. A runner doesn't win the race without training, and a job seeker doesn't get an interview without laying some groundwork. Preparation, not impressive credentials, is the real key to success.

Good preparation begins with understanding the conditions and contexts of the job search. It is the difference between firing out resumes in great quantities with little focus, and taking a few well aimed shots directly at your desired targets. Your success rate will increase markedly if you do preliminary research before sending out your applications.

Say you learn from a friend who works at your dream company that the perfect position has just opened up. You quickly cut and paste your cover letter and resume into an e-mail, and then wait with baited breath. Every time the phone rings, you race to answer it, confident it will be the company calling for an interview. So it comes as somewhat of a shock when you hear that someone else got the interview you so coveted. With your high grades and impressive work experience, why wouldn't the company so much as give you a shot?

When your friend tells you later that the person who "stole your interview" had impressed the boss with a cover letter that showed she'd thoroughly researched the company, you feel like kicking yourself. If only you had done your research instead of sending out the same cover letter and resume you send to everyone.

Research is so essential to your job search that it cannot be overemphasized. Recruiters and hiring managers consistently report that candidates who seem informed about the organization and the industry are given priority in the initial review of applications, and are most likely to succeed later at the interview stage. Almost every company will ask the question, "Why us?" Doing research ensures you can answer this question in an educated fashion. You'll have a great advantage over your competition if you are able to express an understanding of the objectives of the organization (products, services, or operations), the company culture, and why your skills and experience are ideally suited to their needs.

Three Steps for Effective Research

The better the information you gather, the more on target your cover letter and resume will be. The key to successful investigation is knowing what to look for and where to find it. The following three steps will guide you through this all-important research process:

1. Deconstruct the job description.

2. Contemplate the company

3. Investigate the industry.

Step 1: Deconstruct the Job Description

Make a list of the employer's desired skills and qualifications for the position you seek. (The exercise at the end of this chapter gives you a chance to practice doing just this.) And ask yourself the following questions:

- How did you learn of the position opening?
- Who is the company trying to target as its source of qualified candidates?
- Do you have an "in" from whom you can get the inside scoop about the firm's search?
- Have you seen resumes of other professionals in the field?
- Do you have an understanding of what may be standard information to include in your resume, or formatting preferences?

Many business-related fields will emphasize the traditional chronological resume, whereas arts or communications organizations will be open to other styles; finding out which you should use before you get started will spare you a lot of time and heartache.

Step 2: Contemplate the Company

Look into the firm's noted areas of strength and focus to find out in which industries or product areas it excels. Also, explore the following:

- How does this job support the other functions of the department, division, and overall organizational structure?
- What effect does the position have on other departments and what are their functions and structures?
- What are the company's stated goals and mission?
- What is the corporate culture?
- How stable is the company?
- Who are its competitors?

Step 3: Investigate the Industry

Be sure to find and flesh out answers for the following:

- What are the latest developments in the field or industry?
- How is the current economy affecting the field?
- What trends are being forecast?

All of this information should influence the way in which you construct your approach to the job search and the content of your resume and cover letter. The more knowledgeable you are, the clearer you will be about your potential role and the better you will impress employers of your ability to contribute to their organization. Without proper background research, your cover letter and resume will be a shot in the dark. You could get lucky, but why not illuminate the playing field?

Researching is so often overlooked by candidates that it is your "secret weapon" to getting your application to the top of the heap. Recruiters and hiring managers unanimously express interest in the candidate who has done his or her research, for several reasons:

- The candidate does the legwork for the employer by pointing to the match between candidate's qualifications and their needs.
- The candidate demonstrates knowledge of, and interest in, the company, putting him ahead of the more generic applications that do not directly address the company's goals.
- The candidate's knowledge of the organization or company results in a higher likelihood of retention if hired, an advantage for avoiding future costly and time-consuming replacement searches.

Where to Look

So, how exactly did that classmate or coworker "steal" your interview out from under your nose? Probably it was that she was creative in her research. She went to the library, looked on the Internet, and visited her career center—all things you could have done if you'd taken the time.

The bottom line? The information that will make your resume and cover letter sparkle is out there; it's up to you to find it and make the most of it. Employer websites are a great place to start. Most provide instructions for submitting resumes and applying for jobs—this can help you determine how to focus your efforts in your application. To find out more about a specific employer, a position, or an industry, consult as many resources as are available to you. Go to the library, search the Web, call your dad, talk to your friends, attend networking events, contact your alma mater.

Here are some websites insiders recommend to jumpstart your investigation:

- To get in-depth information on some of the top hirers in the United States, check out WetFeet's Industry and Company Profiles (www.wetfeet.com).

- Catch up on the latest news about the company and industry you're interested in at PR Newswire (www.prnewswire.com), NewsDirectory.com, and the Business Times (www.bizjournals.com).

- America's Career InfoNet (brought to you by the U.S. Department of Labor) features helpful information on wages and employment trends (www.acinet.org).

- The Occupational Outlook Handbook from the U.S. Bureau of Labor Statistics (www.bls.gov/oco/home.htm) provides career and occupational information for various fields.

- WetFeet's Real People Profiles (www.wetfeet.com) give an insider's view of work in a wide range of fields.

Networking

Nothing is better than having an "in" with the company where you're applying. Before you prepare your resume and cover letter, get in touch with someone who can help answer questions regarding what makes a good candidate. If you don't know someone on the "inside," try to make contact through personal networks or through professional associations.

You can find contact information on associations in almost every field or industry via the online directory provided by the American Society of Association Executives (www.asaenet.org) and the Internet Public Library's Database (www.ipl.org).

Why Research?

Imagine for a moment that you are the CEO of your dream company and want to hire one or more new employees. When you've got the pick of the litter, whom do you choose? Certainly you would want someone who has shown a genuine interest in your company by taking the time to learn about it and figure out how they could make it even better. Yes, your ideal future employee would take the job seriously, and perhaps even work for the company for years to come. Clearly the candidate who's done the research is going to get the job.

But it's not just for the employer's sake that you should research. To be genuinely enthusiastic, you need to know for yourself why the employer interests you. The company's primary industry, group, or specialty may be right

in line with your career goals. Or you may be most excited by the company's standing in its field. Perhaps a discussion with a current employee about the company culture generates your interest. Every job and every company offer differing opportunities for accomplishment; each will have various pros and cons. Take advantage of research to clarify your own goals and priorities. Then use the information to find the right place in which you can succeed.

If the employer cannot identify why you would want the position and how you would benefit (besides the paycheck), they will not believe you are applying with serious intent. They will pass over your resume in favor of someone who has clearly articulated how his or her career goals will be furthered by the position. This is often why an "overqualified" candidate's application gets put into the "no" pile. Career changers and job searchers who are worried about appearing "overqualified" will benefit by stressing their goals for exposure to a new field. This approach allows candidates who have held great responsibility in prior jobs to persuasively apply to a range of new positions. Whatever the case, make sure that your resume and cover letter accurately reflect your interests and show that you've done your homework.

One more time, with feeling: Before submitting a cover letter and resume to a potential employer, gather ammunition: information and insights (based on your research and self-assessment) that will target your "pitch" to exactly meet your prospective employer's goals.

Top Five Things That Will Automatically Screen out an Applicant
5. Resume sent without indication of what you are applying for
4. Poor quality materials, including photocopies, handwritten, or typed applications
3. Not demonstrating the right qualifications for the position
2. Too many pages of reading
1. Misspelling, poor editing, and bad grammar

WetFeet®

"Bottom Line" Skills

Say you had the opportunity to go back, to have another chance at writing the killer cover letter for snagging that dream job. Would you emphasize certain basic skills and qualities that every employer wants? Is there anything you could have done to make yourself a more attractive candidate? In figuring out the "bottom line" skills that employers are looking for, take a look at some recent data from the National Association of Colleges and Employers (NACE):

- What qualities do employers want most from the college students they consider candidates for employment? Communication skills, honesty and integrity, and teamwork skills are at the top of the list, according to respondents to a survey conducted by the National Association of Colleges and Employers (NACE).

- Employers responding to NACE's *Job Outlook 2003* survey were asked to rate the importance of candidate qualities and skills on a five-point scale, with five being "extremely important" and one being "not important." Communication skills (4.7 average), honesty/integrity (4.7), teamwork skills (4.6), interpersonal skills (4.5), motivation/initiative (4.5), and strong work ethic (4.5) were the most desired characteristics.

- The majority of the respondents of this survey (52 percent) were service-sector employers. 36.4 percent were manufacturers, and 8.2 percent were government/non-profit employers. (An additional 3.4 percent could not be classified by sector.)

To find out more about the NACE *Job Outlook 2003* survey, please see the resource section at the end of this guide, or visit www.naceweb.org.

Effective self-promotion begins with understanding an employer's vision of an attractive candidate. Your cover letter and resume must communicate your ability to deliver the desired goods. What do you have to tempt an employer? If you don't know, it's time to learn how to assess and articulate your particular strengths.

Determining What You Have to Offer

Ever get stuck watching Uncle Fred's travel slides? Time ticks mercilessly by as Fred displays endless photos while giving blow-by-blow descriptions of people you will never meet and places you'd never want to visit. Whatever you do, do not let your cover letter and resume become like Uncle Fred's pictures. Always keep your audience in mind, and only include the highlights of your experiences.

Before you begin writing, have a good look at yourself. Which elements of your years of wisdom, experience, and accomplishment belong on a couple of sheets of paper, and which don't? What characteristics make you stand out from the crowd but also show that you're a team player? What kind of candidate does your target employer usually hire? Be prepared to think through your activities and achievements and tell your compelling life story in one to two pages.

In addition to knowing all of the factual information about yourself—including grades, test scores, and dates of employment—think about how to portray yourself in a positive, confident light while telling the true story of who you are and what you've accomplished. You must have insight into your strengths and weaknesses to create a compelling letter and resume.

Here are some of the best sources for inspiration:

Academic records. Gather your school transcripts, standardized test scores, scholarship applications and awards, and any other information that may help you paint a picture of your academic capability. Calculate your GPA, because you might need this information at some point. If you are concerned about

your GPA, calculate it using several cuts—overall, major-only, or by year—to see which provides the most favorable view to note on your resume, or at least mention in the interview if asked. Always use a standard 4.0 scale.

Recommendations. Re-read any recommendations written for you—for school, jobs, or contests. Make note of the strengths mentioned. You can highlight these strengths as you describe your experience and accomplishments in your cover letter and resume.

Performance reviews. Employer reviews may contain information on your rating vis-à-vis your peers. They may also include assessments of your accomplishments during your tenure. They are a good source of strengths and possibly of some quantitative results you've achieved in your career.

Employment history. Prepare a chronological history of the major jobs you've held. Include the company names, your titles, managers' names, the time you spent in those positions, starting and ending salaries, and primary responsibilities. This will be very useful in identifying upward trends in your career—increasing responsibility, increasing salary, or other advancement. Your employment history will also help you identify any gaps that will need to be accounted for on the resume or in the interview.

Top accomplishments. List the most significant accomplishments from your professional, academic, and personal experiences. Write down each achievement; then explain why it is significant to you, how you achieved it, how others helped you, and how you measure its success. You will need to include information about at least two of your top accomplishments in your resume, preferably with an indication of the results achieved. Later on in this guide, we include an exercise to help you articulate your accomplishments for the cover letter and resume.

Survey your strengths. Once you've got a handle on the facts of your career and education, you're in a good place to think about the types of work or activities in which you've performed well and felt good about it. The skills you used in these situations are most likely some of your strengths. Include evidence of these on your resume so the reader can identify you as a strong analyst, born leader, or formidable writer. Since these areas will likely be explored further in your interviews, think through how you might talk about some examples from your resume.

Address your limitations. You obviously won't highlight your weaknesses in your cover letter or resume, but omission of information might prompt a resume reviewer to question these areas. If your resume lacks information on leadership positions, for example, you may need to show strengths in several other areas. If you don't know the computer applications specified in the job description, you might emphasize that you are a quick learner and familiar with comparable programs.

Determine your work values. Loyalty, growth of responsibilities, employee involvement, loosely or clearly defined job functions, teamwork, autonomy, community, competition—some combination of these values (and others) will define corporate culture or organizational atmosphere. Do your values match those of your prospective employers? How have you demonstrated a commitment to the values expressed by the company (either stated directly in the position listing or through your research on their policies)? The cover letter is the ideal place to present your work-related values and how they support the organizations you are pursuing.

Analyzing Your Transferable Skills

How many times have you seen "excellent communication skills" listed as a required qualification in a job description? Certain capabilities are crucial for succeeding as a professional, no matter what the field. The beauty of these core skills is that you can acquire them from work in one field, setting, or academic experience, and apply them to another. For this reason, these skills are often called "transferable skills." Communication, teamwork, management, leadership, initiative, adaptability, analytical, and organizational skills are valued across many fields and can be developed through education, employment, volunteer activities, and hobbies.

This section reviews employers' most sought-out attributes in a broad spectrum of industries. Which you choose to highlight depends on the particular requirements of a position and the corporate culture of each company you're targeting. The list of questions following each skill set will help you identify your relevant skills and how you accomplished them. These questions should also help you see that skills or expertise developed in one context can help you prepare for a successful career in another.

Quantitative and Analytical Ability

Quantitative or analytical skills are critical components of many jobs, particularly in business and scientific fields. They are fundamental to your success in industries such as financial services and consulting, especially during the first few years of your career. In these fields, if you show no evidence of these skills, you will not get to the interview.

Have You:

- Filtered through data and assumptions and identified reasonable responses to complex problems?

- Synthesized large amounts of information and identified issues?

- Identified a problem and taken a proactive approach to solving it?

- Done well in courses with heavy analytical and quantitative content?

- Performed experiments that required formulation of a hypothesis and collection of evidence to prove or disprove it?

- Taken courses in mathematics, statistics, or other subjects that utilize analytical thinking?

If so, you may have the quantitative or analytical ability employers look for.

Drive for Results (Initiative)

An increasing number of companies and non-profit organizations are emphasizing results in their hiring needs. Employers in any field want to know whether you have the ambition, motivation, attention to detail, and energy necessary to deliver real results.

Have You:

- Brought new customers or revenue into your company? Developed new programs or initiatives?

- Proven yourself as a self-starter who goes above and beyond requirements?

- Shown the ability to switch priorities and move quickly among different tasks?

- Set a challenging goal and achieved it?

- Attended to the details while juggling multiple tasks?

- Taken an innovative and/or efficient approach to getting something done?

The need for specific, often quantitative, measurements of your accomplishments should start you thinking about how to track and measure your achievements if you don't do that already.

Achievement/Intellectual Capacity

Are you outstanding in any of your accomplishments? Employers may be interested in someone who can achieve beyond the norm, or who can demonstrate ambition in their endeavors.

Have You:

- Earned honors or awards?
- Received academic scholarships or fellowships?
- Taken on challenging courses or a heavy workload?
- Pursued intellectual activities (chess, computer programming, etc)?
- Attended academically rigorous schools?
- Done well on standardized tests (SAT, GMAT, LSAT, and so on)?
- Earned a high GPA?
- Received awards and recognition in the workplace?

Leadership

Leadership can be expressed both through your managerial experiences and through your willingness to take on responsibility, even if your role is not that of a supervisor or team captain. Many employers look for leadership qualities in their staff.

Have You:

- Managed people?

- Facilitated meetings?

- Led teams in solving problems?

- Coordinated outside vendors?

- Held a leadership position in a school organization, team, or club?

- Been elected to a post by your peers?

- Organized or coordinated significant events?

- Had a position of significant responsibility with a previous employer?

- Hired or fired anyone?

Teamwork

Teamwork with clients and/or colleagues is a critical component of most work environments. Employers look for people who can work effectively with others and inspire them toward a common goal. This means an ability to communicate clearly and collaboratively with managers, peers, assistants, clients, vendors, and anyone you will have contact with through your work.

Have You:

- Been a member of a sports team, study group, or committee?

- Worked effectively with people whose work style or cultural background differ from yours?

- Inspired others to take action in an unstructured situation?

- Taken on the role of a team leader or player as needed?

Of course, you have. We don't know of any candidate, particularly ones with high levels of academic training, who hasn't been involved in working with a team. (Gotta love those study groups!). Identify the teams and/or groups

you've been a part of and think about the role you typically play. Employers may want to hear about your ability to make productive contributions, the type of role you tend to play on a team, or how you've worked with a team to identify and solve a problem.

Industry and Functional Expertise

If you have a strong understanding of an industry though experience or academic training, highlight this in your cover letter and resume. Of course, each industry varies in which insider skills are most important. Here are some useful ways you can think about your knowledge and past exposure.

Have You:

- Worked in an industry for a good chunk of time?

- Held various roles within one industry?

- Held similar functional roles in different industries? Been able to apply your functional knowledge from one industry to another?

- Written a thesis or research paper about a particular industry, business issue, or other topic?

- Volunteered in a particular field, or followed current events related to an industry or issue?

- Participated in conventions, conferences, symposiums, or associations in a specific field?

- Developed specialized skills—such as technical, industry based, administrative, or in-depth knowledge from your academic training?

Unlike Uncle Fred's approach to sharing past exploits, you can carefully develop focused descriptions of the most interesting and valuable of your experiences to share with recruiters and hiring managers. The goal of assessing your skills is being able to identify what you can offer an employer, and demonstrate how hiring you will help a company meet its objectives.

Exercises

The ability to communicate your abilities, skills, and goals are key to creating persuasive job search materials. Try your hand at the following exercises as a means of effectively organizing and expressing your qualifications.

Exercise 1: Skill List

Review the following list of skills and circle or highlight the competencies you have demonstrated in your work, academic, or personal experiences. These skills are organized in categories representing some of the major core skill areas sought by employers. Use the extra spaces to write down additional skills for each of the various categories.

Prepare Your Skill List

Communication	Teamwork	Managerial	Leadership
explained	collaborated	directed	facilitated
interpreted	cooperated	supervised	led
mediated	coordinated	delegated	instructed
negotiated	assisted	managed	coached
reported	supported	ran	guided
corresponded	backed	oversaw	motivated
drafted	shared	hired	piloted
edited	participated	administered	taught
composed	contributed	executed	enabled

Initiative	Adaptability	Analytical	Organizational
created	anticipated	investigated	administered
expanded	improved	examined	arranged
launched	changed	researched	compiled
designed	negotiated	surveyed	coordinated
established	learned	calculated	maintained
devised	adapted	appraised	managed
instituted	trained	analyzed	operated
developed	complied	evaluated	prioritized
generated	modified	examined	processed

On Your Mark

Exercise 2: Achievement Statements

Having a firm grasp on your experiences and competencies won't do you a lick of good if you can't convey them to employers in a concise and effective way. The format of a cover letter and resume gives you a mere two or three pages in which to express your qualifications. Your job is to make those pages engaging and action-packed. Every word counts. For each bullet point stating what you've done, you'll want to lead with a verb and say in as few carefully chosen words as possible what action was taken, in what setting, with what skills, and with what results. This next exercise will walk you through the process of creating achievements statements that really achieve.

 Achievement Statement Example

Environmental Advocate, Sierra Club: Designed and implemented a campaign strategy to educate the public about climate change and shape international treaties on the issue. Generated more than $25,000 in new memberships and donations to support the campaign.

Action: campaigned for environmental organization

Setting: worked with the public

Skills: defined goals, designed campaign, implemented campaign, conducted outreach, educated public

Results: improved public awareness of issues, increased visibility of organization, generated 500 new members ($5,000 revenue), acquired $20,000 in donations

Now it's your turn to try!

Write Your Own Achievement Statements

Use this workbook to practice writing your own achievement statements.

Action: _____

Setting: _____

Skills: _____

_____

_____

Results: _____

_____

_____

Situation (job, academic, personal): _____

_____

_____

_____

Statement: _____

_____

_____

_____

_____

_____

_____

Exercise 3: Objective Statement

📄 Writing an Objective Statement

Part I

An objective statement can help you clarify and convey your immediate career goals. Write down the kinds of positions, types of organizations or settings, and which skills you want to use or develop in your next job.

Position Desired: _____

Setting: _____

Skills or Goals: _____

_____

_____

_____

Part II

Now practice putting the information generated in Part I of this exercise into objective statements you can use in your resume or cover letter. Below are some suggested phrases to get you started.

Seeking a challenging _____ **position in the** _____

field, that offers an opportunity to _____

_____

_____.

Writing an Objective Statement . . . continued

To use my _____, _____, and _____

skills in a position as a _____.

_____

_____

A career position that would build on my experiences as _____,

while contributing to _____.

_____

_____

Seeking an entry-level opportunity in _____.

_____

_____

To provide _____ to an organization that _____.

_____

_____

Exercise 4: Job Description

Now that you are able to identify your skills, create active achievement statements, and clearly state your career objectives or goals, you are *almost* ready to respond effectively to the job openings that interest you. The final crucial step is to become an expert at identifying employers' needs and demonstrating the correspondence of those needs to what you bring to the table.

Convincing employers that you have relevant qualifications greatly increases your chances for getting an interview. Respond to as much of the job listing as possible by creating a checklist of the employer's stated needs, and matching it as directly as possible to the descriptions in your cover letter and resume.

Analyzing a Job Description

Have a look at the following sample, based on a real advertisement on an online job board. The italicized words form the basis for shaping your application materials.

Sports Marketing Internship

Are you interested in a *career in marketing*? Have you recently completed a marathon, triathlon, century ride or are you just an *avid sports participant*? We are looking for an *energetic, active* person to join our marketing team in a summer internship that will be rewarding, educational, and will provide all of the excitement of crossing the finish line after months of training!

About the Internship:

The intern will *assist* in general marketing tasks from *program creation and implementation to preparing materials for programs/events*. He/she will help out

---

with general *marketing office duties*, and will help out at field and in-store *events*. The marketing intern will have some in-store tasks as well, in order to *learn all aspects of marketing in a retail environment*. Some roles and responsibility will fluctuate as help is needed in other areas.

Qualifications:

- *A background in marketing, with related experience*
- *An active lifestyle*
- *Excellent communication skills*
- *Outgoing and energetic (a "people" person)*
- *MS Office skills*
- *Illustrator* .

About Our Company:

We are a *small, innovative, and growing company* with a retail store and an online site. We cater to athletes of all levels and provide the best brands in sports apparel at great prices. Our *grass roots marketing strategy* keeps us very well *connected* to the active community, and we are always on the go. However, we are much more than just a store with weekly programs and events geared toward *educating and benefiting our customers*. Our *team members are as active* as our customers, participating in events right next to them. For more information please see our website.

Schedule will be 20–30 hours a week, with some evening and/or weekend event work. You MUST have a *flexible* schedule!

Here's what the perfect candidate looks like:

Goals: career in marketing, learn about all aspects of retail marketing

Personal qualities: energetic, active, flexible, outgoing, good communicator, sports lover

Experiences that reflect the ability to assist others, create, implement, serve at events, work as part of a team, utilize computers, understand sports

Interested in the company because: innovative, growing, customer-focused, team-oriented, energetic, and active environment

To demonstrate that your interests, goals, and skills are exactly what the employer is looking for, feel free to use the same words found in the job posting in your cover letter or resume. Synonyms work well, too.

WetFeet®

Practice Analyzing a Job Description

Now you give it a try. Print out a job posting that catches your eye. Highlight or circle the relevant words and phrases, and use them to fill in the spaces below.

Goals: _____

_____

_____

Personal qualities: _____

_____

_____

Experiences that reflect ability to: _____

_____

_____

Interested in the company because: _____

_____

_____

Time to Get Cookin'

- Customizing Cover Letters

- General Formatting Guidelines

- Sample Cover Letters

Customizing Cover Letters

By now, you should know which ingredients make up an appealing job application. If you are going to prepare an irresistible entrée, you'll need to have an understanding of the employers' "taste" in employees—qualifications, skills, and fit with the corporate culture—and you'll need to know what's in your pantry—the achievements and skills available to you for seasoning your application. The prep work is done. Now it's time to get cooking. Fortunately, when it comes to cover letters, there is a basic recipe to follow. Once you learn it, you'll be able to vary your approach to suit each position, industry, and employers' preferences.

There are two basic types of cover letters: Those developed to respond to a specific job opening and those that serve as letters of introduction. The latter is sometimes called a broadcast letter, and it can function like a "cold call" to develop opportunities where no immediate job opening may already exist. Like a good appetizer, all cover letters have one main purpose: to whet the reader's appetite, get them interested enough to move on to your resume and subsequently want to interview you. In many cases, the cover letter is the first thing the employer encounters about you, so make this first impression a good one. If the letter does not have a hook that makes the reader curious to know more, your resume will not even get a glance.

While your cover letters should follow a basic structure, it's best to avoid creating a form letter. After developing a basic outline, your goal is to entice employers with a clear, concise, and well thought-out summary that suggests you offer exactly what they need.

Here's what every cover letter should include:

Basic Cover Letter

- Your contact information

- Date

- Employer's contact information

- Paragraph 1—introduction (why you are writing)

- Paragraph 2—what you offer them

- Paragraph 3—why you want to work with them

- Paragraph 4—what happens next

- Closing

This structure contains all of the information you will need to tempt a recruiter to review your resume, whether you are applying to a specific opening or are initiating contact with a firm that is not advertising opportunities. The basic structure of the cover letter will provide a frame upon which you can build the letter to conform as closely as possible to the requirements and preferences of the targeted employer.

Avoid "canned" letters! Recruiters and hiring managers tell us that formulaic letters often end up in the "no" pile. The applicant who customizes his or her words is more appealing, and will be given preference over others. One insider puts it this way: "The cover letter is the one opportunity they have to talk to me." Employers don't want to waste their time on a candidate who is not genuinely interested in the position and their company.

General Formatting Guidelines

In cooking, basic ingredients form the start of a good dish, but the way you combine the ingredients also impacts the outcome of your efforts. The same is true for your cover letter. Careful choice of words, tone, and aesthetics are essential to creating a pleasing product.

The "write" stuff. Insiders tell us that cover letters are used to assess an applicant's ability to write clearly and concisely. For example, candidates with strong technical focus and international candidates seeking a position in the United States whose first language is not English undergo this type of scrutiny. As with your resume, be sure to proofread for typos.

Lookin' good. To increase the professional look of your application, use the same paper, contact information, header, and font style in both your cover letter and resume. It is acceptable (and often encouraged) to e-mail applications. For more on this, see the "Sending your Application Materials" section later in this guide.

A well-tuned tone. The tone of your cover letter in most circumstances will be professional but thoughtful, persuasive but restrained. Use concise sentences and be direct. At the same time, be sure to inject plenty of enthusiasm and genuine interest into your letter.

Custom content. In your cover letter, include information that truly tailors the application to a particular employer and specific job opening. Complement and reinforce the qualifications presented in your resume, using words and phrases from the employer's job listing and/or website.

Here are some points about content you'll want to keep in mind as you write your letter:

1. How you learned of the job or company is important to recruiters and hiring managers, especially if there exists a mutual connection that can speak of your qualifications.

2. Demonstrate a good fit with the employer's corporate or organizational culture. Be sure to back up any assertions of personal characteristics by describing the resulting achievement either on your resume or in your cover letter. Ideally, the cover letter refers to information found on your resume without being repetitive or redundant.

3. Go beyond the resume in explaining your situation and career direction. For example: "My career goals include gaining leadership experience in the delivery of financial advising services and working in a private business setting that supports high-quality customer care. I will be able to relocate for this kind of opportunity."

4. Avoid discussing weaknesses or making excuses; instead, explain your situation in a way that indicates a sense of purpose and that you have learned something of value from your experiences. For example, if you have been laid off, what have you done to be productive since losing the job (e.g. volunteering your time with a worthy cause, reaffirming or reshaping your career goals)?

5. If salary requirements are requested in a job posting, discuss them in your cover letter. It's best not to trap yourself by naming a very specific amount. Instead, say something such as "my salary requirements are in step with the responsibilities of the position and the expertise I would offer your company."

Finally, in some fields such as investment banking or consulting, the cover letter is a little like a bull market—it's taken for granted until there's a problem. This can also be true when job searching through an on-campus recruiting process. Where this may be the case, we recommend a low-risk strategy. The cover letter should be kept short and to the point, with a maximum length of one-half page. Be sure to include all of your critical information in your resume, because there's a good chance your cover letter won't be read.

Top Five Things Interviewers Look for in a Cover Letter
5. "Readability"
4. A sense of the applicant's personality
3. How an applicant found out about the job opening
2. Something eye-catching
1. Evidence that the applicant has researched the company

Time to Get Cookin'

Sample Cover Letters

Now it's time to see how all the pieces discussed in the first chapter come together. The letters in this section demonstrate a variety of formats, fields, and professional levels. Don't take the examples here as prescriptions. Instead, use them to provide you with ideas for creating concise correspondence that reflects your strengths. These letters contain fictionalized names and organizations, but the information is based on real work histories and position listings.

A Specific Position

Although somewhat lengthy, this letter does a thorough job of emphasizing the relevant skills and goals of the applicant. Note that it is directed towards Human Resources and therefore includes the job number as a subject header. Ideally, addressing an individual is preferable than just going with "Human Resources Administrator"; you can call the organization to inquire about the hiring person's name and title.

LETICIA ROBERTS
Address
City, state, zip
Telephone
E-mail

June 10, 2003
World Art Museum
200 Lafayette Street
San Francisco, CA 94100
FAX: 415.555-9410

RE: Position # 436654, Membership Assistant

Dear Human Resources Administrator:

I am applying to the position of Membership Assistant with the World Art Museum. I learned of the opportunity through your online posting on Craigslist.org, and feel my qualifications are a good match for the responsibilities of the position.

I have several years of customer service and administrative experience in the non-profit community. As Member Services Assistant for the International Association of Business Communicators (IABC), I responded to daily requests for the association's library services department, providing publication information and resource referrals to association members and the public. I was also responsible for editing informational and promotional materials, as well as preparing for and working on-site at the association's annual international conference. As Office Support Person for the ASPECT Foundation, I processed applications to the organization's study abroad program, distributed program

Time to Get Cookin'

materials to applicants, and used Microsoft Word and Excel programs extensively. These duties required strong communication skills, attention to detail, and an ability to both organize and prioritize several tasks at once.

I am very interested in education and the arts. At Bryn Mawr College, I took courses in both art and art history, and I participated in an educational exchange program through which I studied Renaissance art in Florence, Italy. Since then, I have taken extension courses through UC Berkeley in Asian and Latin American art history.

As a result of these experiences, I am enthusiastic about continuing to work with non-profits, and would like to further explore career possibilities with public arts organizations. A position as Membership Assistant with the World Art Museum would combine my member service and clerical skills, my interests and my career goals. I am confident I can be of value to your organization and the customers you serve. Please feel free to call me to set up an interview, or if you need more information. I look forward to hearing from you.

Sincerely,

Leticia Roberts

[Enclosure]

Personal Contact

The letter on the opposite page is quick and to the point. The introduction can be brief, as the employer has already heard of the candidate through their mutual contact. Note that the employer is addressed by her first name; only do this if your contact has suggested it is appropriate. When in doubt, include the full name and title of your addressee.

Bill Pendleton
Address
City, state, zip code
Telephone
E-mail

June 14, 2003

Cathy Stevenson
McKinsey & Company
75 Park Plaza, 3rd Floor
Boston, MA 02116-3934

Dear Cathy,

Frank William suggested that I forward my resume to you for your consideration. I am a second-year MBA student at the Krannert Graduate School of Management at Purdue University, and I am currently working as a summer associate at Motorola in Chicago.

As Frank may have mentioned, I am in the top 5% of my class at Krannert, and I was recently elected President of the MBA student body. In and out of the classroom, I have consistently demonstrated my capacity to make a positive impact regardless of the situation. My analytical and personal skills are ideally suited to management consulting, and I am confident that I would be an asset to McKinsey & Company.

I will call you next Wednesday to discuss next steps. If you have any questions regarding my resume or qualifications, please do not hesitate to call. I look forward to speaking with you.

Sincerely,

Bill Pendleton

[Enclosure]

Broadcast Letter

In the letter on the opposite page, Linda emphasizes her personal qualities, as well as some of her background. This letter style is assertive, and will be most effective if she has done a good job of researching the qualities this firm looks for in its candidates. The conclusion suggests a very proactive approach to targeting the prospective employer and requires follow-through.

LINDA S. BRADFORD
305 Locust Drive #12
Los Angeles, CA 90046
310-555-0883

August 30, 2000

Hamilton Trout
Andersen Consulting
Spear Street Tower
One Market Plaza
Suite 3700
San Francisco, CA 94105

Dear Hamilton:

I am writing to introduce myself as a candidate for a consulting position at your firm. I have excellent academic and professional credentials, as indicated on my enclosed resume. Throughout my professional career, I have adhered to the highest standards of excellence and have demonstrated strong communication skills, analytical ability, poise, creativity, and dedication.

Andersen's excellent reputation and corporate clientele are an ideal match with my interests. In particular, I believe my experience in formulating legal strategies and preparing analyses for complex litigation cases would be an excellent addition to your Strategic Services Competency Group.

I plan to be in San Francisco the week of September 15 and would like to meet with you then to further discuss my qualifications. I will call you on Friday and look forward to scheduling a meeting at your convenience in mid-September.

Very truly yours,

Linda S. Bradford

General Cover Letter Outline

This cover letter outline is geared towards responding to a particular position opening. The format could easily be converted to a broadcast letter by changing the first paragraph to:

I am interested in pursuing career opportunities in the _____ [city, state or location] office. I am currently a _____ at _____, and it is with enthusiasm that I ask to contribute my training and experience to your organization.

📄 Cover Letter Format

The following is a general outline for a cover letter that you can use to create your own cover letters.

Your Header

Address, telephone, e-mail

Date

Employer Name
Title
Address

Dear _____,

I am writing to submit my application for a _____ position in the _____ [city, state or location] office. I am currently a _____ at _____, and it is with enthusiasm that I ask to contribute my training and experience to this exciting new position.

Cover Letter Format

I have been a _____ working on _____ for nearly _____ years, and I am committed to pursuing a career in _____. While I have greatly enjoyed and appreciated the opportunity to work at the forefront of these exciting issues while at _____, I feel the need for a personal and professional change. Your organization is poised to _____, and it is truly exciting to see the _____ in your [city-location] office. This position offers the opportunity to participate in _____.

I believe that my work experience makes me well suited to assume the responsibilities of a _____ position. [Give examples.]

As you can see from my resume, my background in _____ extends beyond my work history at _____. As a result of my experiences, I have become a quick learner who _____. [Describe more skills and personal qualities that match the position.]

I would welcome the chance to discuss this opportunity with you at your convenience. If you have any questions or require any additional information, please do not hesitate to contact me via e-mail at _____ or by telephone, ____-____-_____. Thank you very much for your time and consideration. I look forward to hearing from you.

Sincerely,

Your name

_____

[Enclosure]

Resumes and the Recipe for Success

- Focus on Form and Function

- General Formatting Guidelines

- The Guts of Your Resume

- Resume Design and Organization

- Special Cases

- Basic Resume Don'ts and Dos

- Mail Merge Morons and Other Big Offenders

- Sample Resumes

Focus on Form and Function

Once you've wowed 'em with your cover letter, you'll need a resume that will build on that enthusiasm. There are two areas in which you should conform to standard practice: packaging and content. Resume readers prefer to focus more on content, but it's format that enables them to pick out useful information quickly. To assure a good read, both content and format must be in top shape. As a general rule, the resume is not the place to push the envelope. Remember, resume readers may be reviewing hundreds of resumes for a single position. Few of them will give you extra credit for using bright blue paper or including colorful cartoons. If anything, this will get you snubbed in most fields and for most positions. Good resumes are carefully and deliberately organized and to the point—a quick and informative read.

General Formatting Guidelines

So what is the recipe for success with your resume? Stick with a format that's clean, error-free, easy to read, and that clearly shows two main sections: education and experience. The format of your resume has one objective: to make your qualifications easy to understand. When formatting your resume, you should adhere to the three Cs—clean, clear, and concise. In business fields, such as financial services or consulting, add a fourth C, conservative. While

most resume reviewers don't have a specific model in mind, all seem to appreciate a fifth C, consistency. This generally means:

- A single, standard font: Times New Roman, Arial, Helvetica, or similar
- A readable font size: 11- or 12-point preferred, but no smaller than 10
- Neutral paper color: white or off-white
- Standard layout: no more than 1-inch, no less than .5-inch margins, left justified, line spaces between sections
- One or two pages in length
- Aesthetics: white space, symmetry, uniformity
- Clear resume organization: a few sections, labeled clearly, chronological listing with dates, and bulleted points

Bullets, which make information easier to scan, are often favored on resumes. Insiders tell us that reviewers are more likely to toss a resume into the "ding" pile than spend extra time plowing through turgid, clunky prose to find what they're looking for. When you make bulleted points, remember to keep them short (one line if possible) and start them with action verbs.

Resist the temptation to use excessive text formatting, graphics, or graphs. Cuteness of any kind may be perceived as unprofessional. Such extras eat up space that could be dedicated to providing evidence of accomplishments and qualifications. Certainly, there are fields where creativity and artistry are appreciated, but it is better to err on the conservative side when you're not certain.

The Guts of Your Resume

Thank goodness resumes aren't written on stone, especially as you're going to need to customize it for every job or field to which you are applying. If you're planning to target a position in more than one field—for example, you're a recent graduate who is considering teaching abroad or trying for a public policy internship—you will want to develop multiple versions of your resume rather than try to capture all of your skills in one document. (That approach often results in a resume that appears unfocused.) If you really want to get to the interview stage, take time to write a solid resume that's relevant to the type of work you're after.

Three ingredients should always appear in your document:

- Contact information
- Education
- Experience

Other sections (which are addressed in more detail shortly) are optional and should be selected in a manner that best demonstrates how your qualifications fit with the position you're targeting.

Always begin with your contact information. Any objective or summary of skills should follow next. If you're a student, and particularly if you're from a top-ranked school, you will want to follow next with education. As your school days grow distant, employers become much more interested in your professional experience than in the fact that you were editor of your school newspaper, or what your major was. That said, experienced professionals (those a few years or more out of school) should always emphasize work history or experience and save education for last.

Recipe for Success

The particulars of the education and experience sections are detailed next, as well as other kinds of information you may include in your resume.

Contact Information

Your name and how a person can get in touch with you are the most important things to supply to an employer, and the reason why they should head the pages of all resumes. Seems straightforward, but many people make the mistake of sending resumes with old contact information, or omitting telephone numbers and e-mail addresses. Be sure to include the name you use professionally, a home address, and the telephone number or numbers where you are most easily reached. Get an e-mail account if you don't already have one; many employers prefer this method of reaching candidates, including those in nontechnical fields.

Education

This section might be more aptly titled, "Education and Academic Achievement." Information should include schools attended, degrees conferred and when, and other data regarding your time in school such as GPA, SAT, GRE, or GMAT scores, scholarships and awards earned, honor society memberships, and class ranking. List only those things that showcase your strengths. If your statistics aren't going to wow the reader, you might as well save the space for other, more noteworthy details.

Experience

Think of this as the results section, rather than the experience section of your resume. Be short on description of duties and long on verifiable outcomes. Mention the type of work you've done, the methods you used, and the

industries in which you have experience, but all in the context of what you've accomplished. If you can quantify the results of your work, you're one step ahead of the game.

A documented progression of roles and tasks is definitely a good thing. One insider tells us, "I'm less inclined to focus on education and more inclined to focus on maturity—what have they done?" Professional advancement is valued in any field or industry. Your accomplishments build on each other; each skill or responsibility is the foundation for continued growth and the development of expertise. This is true if you are just starting out or are a seasoned professional.

Other (Activities, Additional Skills, Interests)

This area is your opportunity to tell the scanner a little more about yourself and add color to your candidacy. If your efforts have been directed to projects outside of work or academia, they will show up here. Details typically include activities, interests, associations, memberships, and skills not already covered, such as proficiency in foreign languages. Such areas of your life may be relevant to how you will perform on the job—and relevance is the key.

You can also use the Other section to mention activities that hint at gender, race, religion, or sexual orientation. You may have a slight advantage if your activities indicate that you fall into a group that a particular employer is trying to recruit. This is a touchy subject, but many organizations look to recruit a varied workforce to serve an increasingly diverse clientele. Therefore, highlighting your diversity just might help your candidacy.

Insiders tell us that interesting or unusual information in this section can play a significant role in the decision to award an interview. However, take care in the kind of information you dish out. Many people we interviewed say they rejected otherwise decent resumes because of strange mentions in the Other

section. For example, saying you won the Twinkie-eating contest at your fraternity by eating 47 Twinkies in 15 minutes isn't necessarily a selling point if you're trying to break into the financial services industry, or most industries for that matter. Also, be sure to avoid any topics that may be controversial.

Finding Your Focus

You can (and should!) customize your resume in response to every opportunity you pursue. Conventional elements that make up a resume are listed in the table that follows. Think of them as pieces to a puzzle; you must decide the best way to arrange them to demonstrate your value to the company or organization. Be sure to check out the sample resumes in the next chapter to get a sense of how these sections work together.

Common Resume Elements

Element	Description	Benefits/Drawbacks
Contact Information	Name, mailing address, telephone number(s), e-mail address, website.	Employer can see your current location.
Objective	One-sentence summary of your immediate work goals. Objective section follows the contact information at the top of the resume.	Can be too vague or too obvious, or repeat information in the cover letter. Can help add focus to a resume with varied or little experience.
Summary of Qualifications	Provides the top three or four areas from your background you want the employer to focus on.	Adds focus and highlights strengths.
Profile	Professional summary that captures your focus, skills, and expertise in a few sentences.	Particularly good for professionals with a great deal of experience.
Summary of Skills	Lists most relevant skills/keywords for the targeted position.	Helps reader quickly identify your relevant skill areas.
Education	Degree, major, institution, location, date degree conferred. GPA optional.	Most employers want to see this information.
Honors/Awards	Academic, scholarship, recognition for contributions in relevant fields.	Demonstrates leadership or academic achievement.
Certifications, Licensure, Credentials	Important to list if it is a minimum qualification for positions, such as therapists, lifeguards, and engineers.	This information must be current to be useful, especially if licensure is required qualification for position.
Training	Relevant training, continuing education, conference participation.	Shows professional development.
Experience	Can include paid or unpaid positions.	Helpful for those who have little employment; can include any relevant experience.
Employment History	All relevant employment listed in reverse chronological order (most recent first). Must include date, title, employer, and location.	Employers expect to see this information on all resumes.

WetFeet®

Common Resume Elements . . . continued

Element	Description	Benefits/Drawbacks
Internships	Experiential trainings you've had as relevant to skills and qualifications.	Most useful to list for new grads or career changers, or when internship is part of academic curriculum.
Activities/Community Involvement	Volunteer positions, leadership roles, travel abroad, program participation. List dates, titles if any, organization, location.	Shows variety of interests, skills, and accomplishments. Particularly useful if skills are relevant to job.
Language Skills	List only if relevant to the field and you are proficient enough to use your skills on the job. Include level of fluency.	Demonstrates communication competence and multiculturalism.
Technical Skills	Computer programs and lab skills, for example.	Many employers want to see computer competence, even for nontechnical positions.
Research	Includes title, organization, location, project emphasis and outcome, and skills utilized.	Demonstrates specialized knowledge, as well as technical and analytical skills.
Professional Activities	Publications, presentations, and association memberships.	Shows leadership.
Travel	Lists major experiences abroad, dates, and whether travel was through affiliated organizations or independent.	Good for international positions, or to explain time gaps in work history.
Interests	List what you are accomplished at and engaged in.	Gives fuller picture of candidate; controversial interests may not be favorable; takes resume space away from work-related accomplishments.

Recipe for Success

Resume Design and Organization

What's the point of choosing all of the right ingredients to include in your resume, if nobody can read it? Clearly, it's not just what's in the resume that counts, but how the information is presented. Typically, the first glance at your resume will last 30 seconds—and in that time the reader will focus on the first third of the page. This means that the information you most want to share needs to lead your resume. Good design and organization will guide the reader's eyes towards the most important sections and points.

The good news is you don't have to go to design school or even take a class to learn the basics of resume design. Understanding the five basic design layouts, which follow, and their relative strengths will give you the information you need to put together a compelling presentation.

Chronological

This layout lists employment in reverse chronological order—that is, the most recent experience is listed first. The convention for many fields, especially business-related fields, this layout best highlights continuity of experience and work history, shows progression in responsibility, and emphasizes titles and employer names.

 Basic Chronological Layout

Contact info

Education

Date, degree, school

Experience

Date, title, organization (#1)

- Achievement 1
- Achievement 2

Experience

Date, title, organization (#2)

- Achievement 3
- Achievement 4

Additional information

WetFeet®

Copyright 2003 WetFeet, Inc.

Recipe for Success

Functional

This layout, which organizes your experiences by skill sets or industry areas, is particularly suited for career changers and people with little work experience or who have large gaps in work history. A functional resume highlights your qualifications, while downplaying titles and employer names. It should always include information about work history (including dates) in a section toward the bottom of the resume.

 Basic Functional Layout

Contact info

Skill/Experience Group #1

- Achievement 1
- Achievement 2

Skill/Experience Group #2

- Achievement 3
- Achievement 4

Work History

- Date, title, organization #1
- Date, title, organization #2

Education

Date, degree, school

Recipe for Success

Combination

This type of resume includes organizational elements from the chronological or functional layouts, providing the most flexibility in what you can emphasize.

 Combination Layout 1

Contact info

Skill/Experience Group #1

- Date, title, organization (1st)
- Achievement 1
- Date, title, organization (2nd)
- Achievement 2

Skill/Experience Group #2

- Date, title, organization (3rd)
- Achievement 3
- Achievement 4

Work History

- Date, title, organization #1
- Date, title, organization #2

Education

Date, degree, school

Recipe for Success

Combination Layout 2

Contact info

Date, title, organization (1st)

Skill/Experience Group #1

- Achievement 1
- Achievement 2

Skill/Experience Group #2

- Achievement 3

Date, title, organization (2nd)

Skill/Experience Group #3

Work History

- Achievement 4

Education

Date, degree, school

Curriculum Vitae (CV)

Used in science and academia, as well as for some international positions, the CV is a formal list of all professional endeavors. There is no limit to the length of the CV. Objective, summaries, travel, and interests are not typically included.

 Basic CV Layout, page 1

Contact info

Education

Date, degree, school

Skill/Experience Group #1

- Date, title, organization (1st)
- Achievement 1
- Date, title, organization (2nd)
- Achievement 2

Skill/Experience Group #2

- Date, title, organization (3rd)
- Achievement 3
- Date, title, organization (4th)
- Achievement 4

Recipe for Success

Name, Pg 2

Skill/Experience Group #3

- Date, title, organization (2nd)
- Achievement 5

Publications

- Date, title, publisher (1st)
- Date, title, publisher (2nd)

Professional Affiliations

- Date, title, organization (1st)

Honors/Awards

- Date, title, organization (1st)

Recipe for Success

Special Cases

The normal career trajectory used to mean staying with one company or industry and working from entry-level assistant to associate to partner, or some equivalent sequence of duties and titles. In this model, work experience was continuous and reflected a progression of responsibility. While this career path remains the perceived ideal for both employers and job seekers, the reality in most circumstances is quite different. Today's job seekers often hold positions in a variety of settings, begin their careers after taking time to explore their options, or balance personal goals (like the desire to travel or raise children) along with their career pursuits. Employers are currently more open to alternatives to the traditional model of professional development than ever before. Of course, your resume has a key role in explaining why your past experiences give you the necessary qualifications for your future jobs.

While recruiters and hiring managers may be impressed with the assets listed in your resume, they will search for potential red flags to probe during the first interview. In particular, they will look for gaps in qualifications or employment inconsistencies, and may even formulate questions directed at resume weaknesses. Read your resume with a critical eye, looking for things that might appear odd or incongruent—for example, position titles that don't seem to correspond to the duties listed or a series of positions that decrease (rather than increase) in responsibility. Be prepared to address these issues should you get an interview.

Copyright 2003 WetFeet, Inc.

International Aspirations

Many people hope to work for companies based outside the United States or come from abroad seeking opportunities with American firms. Candidates who may be perfectly qualified for a position will be tossed out of the first stages of the application review process because they are uninformed of the differences that play a role in the international job search.

For the international job seeker, preparing winning job application materials goes beyond researching the position, organization, and industry. Candidates must research the typical hiring practices for the country or regions they are targeting. Most non-U.S. positions require a curriculum vitae, which differs from an American resume (and an academic CV) in its length and in that it includes personal information such as age, marital status, and nationality.

Additionally, international job seekers should be able to point to cross-cultural experiences in their background, as well as specialized and functional expertise (often for legal reasons, the employer must be able to prove that a noncitizen is more qualified than every other candidate in the home country). If you are authorized to work abroad legally, you may wish to include this information in your application materials. Finally, you should have a clear grasp of economics and business practices in the country or region you wish to work. So don't be discouraged from pursuing a dream job that's overseas. Just remember that appreciating cultural differences extends to having insight into the expectations of employers in the particular country or region that you would like to be employed.

Lack of Industry Experience

If you suspect that the only people who get interviews are those who have already been in the industry, you're partly right. Certainly, many organizations are biased toward experienced professionals who can "plug in and go." They are relatively safe in assuming that someone who's been in the job before has the skills and characteristics required to do the work. As everyone knows, the best indicator of future performance is past performance. However, employers need to continually bring in new talent as well (the turnover rate is much too high for most organizations to survive on veterans alone). Therefore, if you haven't already developed a track record in the kind of organization, industry, or field you are now pursuing, you should try for the next best thing: demonstrating that you've done the same type of work, albeit in a different context.

How can you do this? As discussed earlier, your resume reviewer will likely be looking for evidence of skills in several areas, such as quantitative and analytical ability, intelligence, drive for results, or teamwork. Think about the things you've done that will showcase your abilities in these areas. Focus on "transferable" skills and experiences you've had that can translate from one industry to another. Additionally, be sure to articulate your career goals clearly and convincingly. Your enthusiasm, willingness to learn, and ability to go the extra mile in your pursuits will make a positive impression on prospective employers.

Time Gaps

One reason recruiters and hiring managers like chronological resumes is that they want to know whether a candidate took time off between school years or jobs. Be prepared to explain any lapses between jobs or between your sophomore and junior year, for example. If you traveled, have ready an explanation of or anecdotes that describe something you learned during that

time. If you took time off to have a baby or resolve a personal issue, you'll probably need to supply that information to the hiring manager. It's usually best not to go into a lot of personal detail—insiders tell us this is a warning sign, especially in the cover letter or first interview. But be clear and focus on what you accomplished during that time. Employers want to be sure you can handle the normal rigors of four or more years in academia, jobs with increasing responsibility, and balancing your personal and professional pursuits.

Job Hopping

If you've been at several companies in just a few years, or never stayed at one company longer than a year or two, you risk being perceived as a job-hopper. Your resume reader may wonder whether you've been fired for poor performance. Frequent career changes sometimes indicate that a person has difficulty sticking with a situation, working through problems, or committing to a job. Many employers look for people who want to stay around for a while— after all, employee turnover is costly in real dollars because of time spent in the search and loss of operational knowledge. However, in today's job market, resume readers are more accustomed to encountering resumes with work histories showing several different employers. If you can clearly articulate how each job has contributed to your professional development and if you can produce strong references, you should have no problem addressing any negative perceptions.

Local Yokels

If you've spent most of your academic and professional life in Boston, an employer may question your sudden interest in joining the Chicago office of a firm. Consider writing about your goals or perspectives on relocating in your cover letter; this can be addressed with the "why you chose them" paragraph.

Be aware that an employer who is thinking about flying you out for an interview will probably quiz you over the phone before ponying up the funds to pay for you to come out for a face-to-face interview.

Portfolio

The portfolio comprises supporting materials that illustrate the accomplishments you outlined in your resume. Conventionally used by artists (to show samples of their artwork) or educators, the portfolio is becoming valuable to many job applicants, especially those aiming for positions in writing, marketing, advertising, and other creative fields. Your portfolio could contain articles by or about you, writing samples, samples of products you've created (including brochures, printouts of Web pages, business plans, and graphical charts), awards or commendations, school papers or transcripts (for current or recent students). In all likelihood, you won't be asked to submit a portfolio in your job application; however, a portfolio can be a very effective tool during an interview—it illustrates and validates the experiences and skills you want to demonstrate to the prospective employer.

 WetFeet Resume Tip

Many insiders tell us they develop interview questions according to experience mentioned on a candidate's resume. The best way to prepare for the first interview is to know your resume extremely well. Develop and practice a 20- to 30-second pitch that summarizes your experience and major achievements You can base this pitch on your objective statements or professional summary/profile. You will use it countless times, to introduce yourself over the phone or in an interview when the interviewer has not had a chance to review your qualifications. Preparing your pitch will help you articulate the items listed on your resume. You should be able to describe points on your resume in a clear, concise, and convincing manner.

Recipe for Success

Basic Resume Don'ts and Dos

So now you've thoroughly researched your employers, have done some soul-searching, and are on the path towards putting together your perfect resume (or resumes). Here are some dos and don'ts to help you avoid common mistakes while building a stronger, more refined resume (and cover letter).

Don't use vague qualitative terms such as "large" or "many," which leave the reader with questions about specifics.

Do use numbers where appropriate to clearly describe your accomplishments, as in "led a team of nine sales reps."

Don't waste resume space with frivolous information, such as "Voted mostly likely to succeed in high school."

Do distinguish the important from the trivial in your background to fit the most relevant and significant elements onto a single page or so.

Don't try to differentiate yourself with unconventional format or tactics such as graphics and colored paper, unless you are applying to arts-related fields.

Do stick to a basic, clear format that helps the reader glean information quickly and with minimal effort.

Don't include reasons for leaving your jobs, salary information, or references on your resume.

Do make your resume a document that focuses on your accomplishments and skills.

Don't try to portray yourself as a jack-of-all-trades in the hope that something will strike the reader's fancy.

Do discuss your two or three most relevant strengths and illustrate them with experience and achievement statements.

Don't get caught in the passive voice trap, writing as if things happened to you. "Went to Argentina to represent the firm . . ."

Do use the active voice with verbs that indicate you're in charge: "Represented firm at international symposium."

Don't refer to yourself as a subject (first or third person) in your resume: "I helped prepare correspondence," or, "Applicant wrote outreach letters to prospective clients."

Do begin each accomplishment statement with an active verb: "Handled all client correspondence"

Don't include e-mail addresses or websites that have the potential to reveal controversial or inappropriate personal information: Avoid addresses such as sxybb@imacutiepie.com or queenoftheraccoons@hotmail.com.

Do present yourself as a professional, with a straightforward e-mail account and Web information that showcases relevant skills and achievements.

Don't include personal information such as social security number, age, race or marital status on your resume.

Do be aware that employers are interested in your eligibility to work legally and may ask for documentation. Take the time to learn about your rights and responsibilities in the workplace.

Don't use your current work e-mail or phone as contact information. This indicates you are job searching on your employer's time, something no prospective employer will view positively.

Do use your current home address, a personal e-mail, and telephone with a professional outgoing message. Be sure that prospective employers can easily reach you; check your messages regularly.

Top Five Things Employers Look for When Reviewing a Resume
5. A well-rounded candidate
4. Something that makes you stand out from all the others who are applying for the job
3. A balance of work (or academic) and life experiences
2. Someone who went to the interviewer's alma mater (not that she's biased)
1. A typo—so the employer can throw it out

Mail Merge Morons and Other Big Offenders

Remember: When slogging through piles and piles of cover letters and resumes, HR recruiters and hiring managers are just looking for a reason to ding you. If your resume or cover letter fits one of these descriptions, you run a high risk of being shuffled into the "no" pile, no matter how strong your background. So beware!

The mail merge moron. Mail merge morons send in their resume and cover letter to Amazon stating how much they would like to work for Barnes and Noble. As one insider tells us, "If they didn't take the time to even read their cover letter before sending it, how will they be able to produce flawless work once they're here?" Three words: proofread, proofread, proofread!

High inflation rates. Yeah, we know, everyone exaggerates to some extent, but insiders tell us that a resume that looks too good to be true probably is. Therefore, most of them look at a glowing resume with a heavy dose of skepticism. You need to sell yourself and showcase your talents without going overboard. The biggest mistake insiders say that jobseekers make is the tendency to overstate experience. "I hate when candidates overstate their actual abilities. Then they get into an interview, and it's a joke. It comes out pretty quickly."

The title titillator. Title titillators think a fancy title will make their experience sound better. One insider encountered a resume where a student's employment included being "CEO," Babysitting Service (there were no other employees). Consider the very impressive-sounding title "Director of Strategic Operations." What on earth

does that mean? Go with "Director of Business Development" instead. When in doubt, simplify so as to make your role and responsibilities clearer, rather than more obscure. Also, be sure that the title you choose is the one that your former employer or reference will confirm you had while at their organization.

The fabricator. Frighteningly enough, many insiders we talked to say they had caught individuals lying about everything from what degrees they had earned to where they had earned them to where they had worked. One remembered a candidate from a top finance school who had lied about being fluent in five languages, one of which was Swedish. It so happened that his first-round interviewer was Swedish. When he began the interview in his native language, the candidate could only blush and admit to lying on his resume. Needless to say, he was not invited back for another interview. Sure you might not get caught, but why take the risk?

Too much of a good thing. Resumes lacking focus are big losers. They include mentions of membership in seven different clubs without a leadership position in any of them; experience in five industries in the past four years; and knowledge of marketing, sales, manufacturing, finance, and information systems. Right! Avoid looking like a dilettante, and groom your resume so it highlights skills and experiences specifically related to your current goals.

Chek you're speling. "A typo is death," as one insider puts it. Our insiders say one typo won't disqualify a candidate, but several typos probably will. On the other hand, any typo is a good enough reason to nix a candidate, and depending on the reader's mood and level of patience, a typo might be just the excuse needed to whittle down that pile. Use your spell checker, but be sure to proofread carefully. Spell checkers won't catch all typos and won't check for other hazards such as misused contractions (your vs. you're, its vs. it's). It's always a good idea to have a friend or two read through your resume before you send it out. Remember, most reviewers are just looking for a reason to throw your resume into the "no" pile.

Technology hang-ups. While many recruiters express a preference for receiving application materials by e-mail, don't expect the person on the receiving end to fumble around with an attached file in a desperate quest to review your qualifications. They are much more likely to move right along to the applicants who have sent their materials in a more accessible form. If you have any doubts about the quality of the format in which your resume will arrive, because of platform or application variables, it's best to send a hard copy as well (In any case, sending a follow-up hard copy shows a little extra initiative and never hurts). Faxing is almost as fast as e-mail, and often more reliable, although it's definitely a good idea to follow up a faxed resume with a phone call to make sure it was received in legible form.

Sample Resumes

Ready to see how all the pieces discussed in the last chapter come together? The resumes in this section demonstrate a variety of formats, fields, and professional levels. The examples here are not intended to be copied exactly, but instead should offer you ideas for creating concise correspondence that reflects your strengths. These letters contain fictionalized names and organizations, but the information is based on real work histories and position listings.

Tutor

This resume, which follows a standard chronological layout, is effective in emphasizing a long and consistent work history. The summary focuses on the long-term experience and excellent results that make up Lee's professional strengths. The subject specializations function as keywords, quickly informing readers of the applicant's areas of expertise.

LEE JONES
Address
Tel · email

Summary of Qualifications

- Over 14 years tutoring adults and children; serving up to 40 ongoing clients annually.

- Develop and teach individualized curriculum based on client abilities and academic goals.

- Strong and enthusiastic recommendations from client families and school staff.

- Proven results: 99% of students increase their standardized test scores in one or more subjects.

SUBJECT SPECIALIZATIONS

- **Standardized Test Preparation:** SAT I & II, SSAT, PSAT, GMAT, GRE

- **Mathematics:** First through twelfth grade – basic arithmetic, pre-algebra, algebra, geometry, trigonometry, pre-calculus

- **English:** Fifth grade through college – spelling, reading, writing

- **Social Sciences:** First grade through college

TUTORING/TEACHING EXPERIENCE

1989-present   **Self-employed as Tutor** in high school and junior high school subject areas

2002   **Instructor,** SSAT Preparation Course, Boston, MA
Designed and implemented curriculum for summer intensive SSAT course for private school students.

1989–1996   **Educational Counselor,** Boston Education Service, Boston, MA
Tutoring of all high school subjects and preparation for SAT with at-risk youth.

1991–1992   **Teacher of English as a Second Language,** International Masters Academy of Britannica, Inc., Tokyo, Japan
Taught English conversation skills to adult students at all proficiency levels.

1989–1991   **Tutor,** A-Level Tutors, Boston, MA
Tutoring on one-to-one basis in many subject areas, from university-level Economics to high school English.

EDUCATION

1988   **B.A. in Economics,** Boston University, Boston, MA

Consulting

This resume, also following a chronological layout, is that of a candidate who is applying for a consulting position. Though Andrew is still in his MBA program, he has chosen to emphasize his work-related experience, placing it at the top of his resume. Because the titles of the first two companies are not self-explanatory, he provides a quick description, adding a clear context to his areas of expertise.

Andrew Wesley Grant
27 Ridge View Way
Wellington, New Zealand
Telephone (Wk) 821 1234 5991 (Hm) 821 1234 2117 (Mobile) 0419 1234 882

EXPERIENCE

1996–Current   **Selecta Multimedia Pty. Ltd.**
New Zealand telecommunications company, $15 billion turnover; 70,000 staff
Marketing Manager, Electronic Commerce
- Managed all marketing for new products involving electronic payments via the Internet, cable, mobile, and basic telephony. Conducted market/industry research, analyzed segments and size, and set up focus groups, positioning, branding, pricing, and promotion strategies.
- Developed Business Case and marketing strategy for Australian and South East Asian markets. The plan was approved and implemented, resulting in an initial market share capture of 15%.
- Managed $500,000 budget.
- Managed cross functional team of eight.

1995–Current   **National Internet Pty. Ltd.**
National Internet Service company providing Dial-up, Web-authoring and consultancy services.
Founder and Managing Director
- Founded and managed national Internet service provider serving more than 5,000 consumer and business accounts.
- Developed and implemented technology and marketing strategies, negotiating contracts with partner companies.
- Raised $500,000 in venture capital and generated profit within 18 months.

1992–1995   **Selecta Corporation**
Senior Business Analyst, Corporate Systems and Processes, Corporate Finance
- Developed Business Cases for new IT systems proposals in consultation with senior national management.
- Identified and wrote associated business requirements, functional specifications, test strategies and training programs in support of business process redesign opportunities resulting in a cost reduction of $50,000 annually.
- Performed complex financial analysis for senior management and Selecta Board, which resulted in changes to the balance sheet.
- Managed three teams across software development life cycle to deliver projects on time and on budget.

1990–1992   **Jervis Partners Pty. Ltd.**
Commodity Traders – Precious and Non-Ferrous Metals
Manager – Commodities Trading and Risk Management
- Identified new markets for buying and selling of commodities globally, resulting in a 15% increase in profits.
- Managed team of five.

EDUCATION

MBA (Technology) – Auckland Business School, University of Auckland
(Studying part-time, working full-time. 15 out of 20 subjects completed.)

BA (Economics) – Royal Military College, Westland University 1985

OTHER

Member of synagogue board of management.
Elected to Student Council, Auckland Business School, University of Auckland.
Interested in chess, classical guitar, current affairs and the Internet.

Banking

This chronological resume emphasizes the candidate's academic training and achievements, including awards and a prestigious school. Clear bullet points, action verbs, and quantifying results all strengthen the presentation of his accomplishments. Although Merrill took time to travel before business school, the gap is nearly undetectable on his resume.

MERRILL MORGAN

Hinman Box 4000 ° Hanover, NH 03755 °603-643-1000 ° merrillmorgan03@dartmouth.edu

EDUCATION

Present   **The Tuck School of Business at Dartmouth College**
Candidate for Master of Business Administration Degree, June 2004
- Tuck Scholar

1992 - 1996   **University of Michigan**
Bachelor of Arts with Distinction
- Double major in Economics and Japanese Studies
- Dean's List, Honors College, Sophomore Honors Award

EXPERIENCE

1998 – 2001   **Lehman Brothers, Inc.**   New York, NY
Proprietary Trader, Listed Equities Division
- Traded $100 mm in public securities on a monthly basis and consistently placed in top 5% in profitability for entire firm.
- Three year profit performance includes positive returns in 31 of 38 months including 29 of final 31 months of active trading.
- Generated over $1 mm in commissions for the firm and promoted to senior trader status after two years.
- Hired, trained and managed a group of eight proprietary traders. Training included equity valuations using fundamental research, buy/sell strategies, and market psychology.
- Trading activity included technical research analysis (e.g. price/volume divergence, momentum and flow charts) to determine optimal purchase and sell points for listed stocks.

1996 – 1998   **J.P. Morgan Securities Corporation**   Chicago, IL
Fixed Income Analyst
- Invested short-term cash management for accounts in excess of $80 million.
- Calculated forward rate information utilizing Excel for comparison with current discount rates, adding 75 basis points value for affected clients.
- Performed risk analysis of portfolios and proper asset allocation.
- Oversaw maintenance of portfolio management software.
- Executed all trades with institutional broker.
- Researched on current trends, news and relevant economic information within the Capital Markets.
- Prepared current market rate information in domestic fixed income markets.
- Verified monthly pricing and yield information on client reports.

1997   **J.P. Morgan Securities Corporation**   Chicago, IL
Summer Intern
- Performed analysis of stock list.
- Analysis assisted in a gain for branch office.

ADDITIONAL INFORMATION
- Licensed Series 7, Series 63 and Series 55
- Interests include: downhill skiing, soccer ping-pong and investing

Undergraduate

A standard chronological layout is employed to emphasize Jose's activities rather than employment history. This layout works well for someone without a lot of work experience, or whose volunteer and personal endeavors reflect more relevance and responsibility than his or her employment. Jose is currently a student and therefore lists education and related coursework on his resume. Additionally, adding an Objective section helps sets the tone for the reader—the information that follows will be viewed in terms of how it supports the objective (in this case, a career in business administration). This format is particularly useful for students and career changers.

Jose Ramirez
jram2@unlv.edu

Permanent Address:
247 Lissom Road
Chicago, IL 30123
(773) 555-1333

Campus Address:
201 Lincoln Ave.
Las Vegas, NV 89154
(702) 444-4444

OBJECTIVE: Summer internship in the field of Business Administration

EDUCATION

University of Nevada, Las Vegas (UNLV)   Fall '01 – present
Bachelor of Arts, expected May 2005
Major: Sociology, *Minor*: Economics, GPA: 3.1
Related Coursework: Microeconomics, Macroeconomics, Probability & Statistics,
Statistical Methods in Economics, Financial Accounting

ACTIVITIES

Undergraduate business society, UNLV   Fall '02 - Spring '03
Developed externship opportunities for sophomores and juniors. Contacted professionals
in financial and consulting firms and made arrangements for student placements. Update
student members on current events pertaining to business opportunities and networking;
sponsor informational seminars, workshops and speakers.

Center For Volunteer Action, UNLV   Fall '01 - Spring '03
Help in local non-profit organizations in Las Vegas. Various short term projects
included: tutored inner-city kids in multiple subjects, refurbished dilapidated
playground and recreational building, solicited food donations and distributed goods to
homeless shelters and soup kitchens.

EXPERIENCE

Intern, **Crate & Barrel**, Chicago, IL   Summer '02
Participated in weekly staff meetings with retail recruiting team, assisted in organizing
summer staff orientations and programs. Created fall schedule for university campus
recruiters. Reserved booths at local college job fairs, and arranged rental car and
hotel accommodations for recruiters.

Server, **Rocket Cafe**, Chicago, IL   Summer '02
Provided friendly customer service in neighborhood restaurant. Worked efficiently as
member of team in all aspects of restaurant operations. Assisted owner/chef in
preparing nightly specials, took customer orders, bussed all tables.

Camp Counselor, **HoopSters Basketball Camp**, Chicago, IL   Summer '01
Supervised and led activities for youth ages 7-11. Assisted basketball coaches in
training and instruction of children.

COMPUTER SKILLS

Familiar with Microsoft Office, HTML, Javascript and internet search engines

Scientific

This is a sample of a curriculum vitae (CV) for a doctoral student in the sciences. The CV is most often used in academia, scientific fields, and for executive-level positions. Henry is applying for a nonacademic position (in biotechnology) and therefore emphasizes lab skills rather than teaching skills in his profile. The CV has no limit to length; therefore, Henry has included all relevant professional accomplishments.

Henry A. I. Yee

Dept. of Cellular & Molecular Pharmacology   Phone: 415.555.2345 (H)
Box 0455   415.555.5555 (W)
.University of California, San Francisco   email: henryy@cgl.ucsf.edu
San Francisco, CA 94143-0455

Profile

Bio-organic / medicinal chemist with experience in synthetic organic chemistry, biochemistry, and molecular and structural biology
- Designed and synthesized myeloid hormone receptor antagonist
- Identified structural determinants of selective myelomimetics

Education

University of California, San Francisco   1996-Present
    Program in Biological Science (PIBS) – Ph.D. program
    Specialization: Biochemistry and Molecular Biology
    Anticipated Graduation Date: February 2003

University of British Columbia   1991-1995
    B.Sc. Combined Honours Chemistry and Biochemistry

Skills

- Chemistry: Multi-step chemical synthesis, water- and air-sensitive reactions, analytical and prep. HPLC, flash chromatography, 1HNMR and 13CNMR spectroscopy>

- Molecular Biology: Transient transfection transactivation assays in mammalian cells, PCR, SDS- PAGE, subcloning and site-directed mutagenesis

- Computer: Irix, Linux and Mac OS X system administration, SYBYL, MidasPlus, Molscript, Raster3D, experienced Macintosh user, some perl and shell scripting and Windows experience

Research Experience

University of California, San Francisco   1997-Present
        Graduate Student
        Research Advisor – Prof. Thomas Smith

Design and Synthesis of Myeloid Hormone Receptor Antagonists
A small molecule myeloid hormone receptor (TR) antagonist was designed by combining the long alkylamide side chain of the estrogen receptor antagonist ICI-164,384 with the myelomimetic GC-1. Several GC-1 analogues with substituents at the carbon atom that bridges the two aromatic rings were prepared via 10 to 14 linear step syntheses. HY-4, the analogue bearing the same side chain as ICI-164,384, was found to bind to MR in vitro and also behave as a competitive antagonist in transactivation assays.

Structural Determinants of Selective Myelomimetics
The structural features of the myelomimetic GC-1 that confer its 10-fold preference for binding to the beta isotype of MR were determined in a study comparing GC-1 to 3,5-dimethyl-3'-isopropyl-L-thyronine (L-DIMIT), the non-selective myelomimetic from which GC-1 was designed. Analogues of GC-1 and DIMIT bearing only one of their two structural differences were synthesized. Receptor binding and transactivation studies of the analogues demonstrate that the oxyacetic acid side chain of GC-1 is the key determinant for its MRb selectivity.

Publications

- Yee, H.A.I., Maynard, J.W., Boxer, J.D. & Smith, T.S. (2003). Structural determinants of selective myelomimetics. *J. Med. Chem., in Press*

- Yee, H.A.I. & Smith, T.S. (2002). Selective myeloid hormone receptor modulators. *Curr. Top. Med. Chem., in press.*

- Yee, H.A.I., Ng, N.H. & Smith, T.S. (2002). Design and synthesis of nuclear hormone receptor ligands. *Methods Enzymol., in press.*

- Yee, H.A.I., Maynard, J.W., Boxer, J.D. & Smith, T.S. (2001). A designed antagonist of the myeloid hormone receptor. *Bioorganic Med. Chem. Lett.* 111, 3821-3825.

- Smith, T.S., Yee, H.A.I., Ng, N.H. & Castelli, G. (2001). Selective myelomimetics: Tissue selective myeloid hormone analogs. *Curr. Op. Drug. Disc. Devel.* 94, 314-322.

- Castelli, G., Ng, N.H., Yee, H.A.I. & Smith, T.S. (2000). Improved synthesis of the iodine-free myelomimetic GC-1. *Bioorganic Med. Chem. Lett.* 101, 3607-3611.

- Yee, H.A.I, Castelli, G., Mitchison, T.J. & Smith, T.S. (1998). An efficient substitution reaction for the preparation of myeloid hormone analogues. *Bioorganic Med. Chem.* 8, 179-183.

- Castelli, G., Maynard, J.W., Yee, H.A.I., Boxer, J.D., Ribeiro, R.C.J. & Smith, T.S. (1998). A high affinity subtype-selective agonist ligand for the myeloid hormone receptor. *Chem. Biol.* 59, 399-406.

- Tanaka, S.H., Yee, H.I., Ho, A.W.C., Lau, F.W., Westh, P. & Koga, Y. (1996). Excess partial molar entropies of alkane-mono-ols in aqueous solutions. *Can. J. Chem.* 714, 3313-3321.

Patents

- Smith, T.S., Yee, H.A.I, Castelli, G., & Mitchison, T.J. (2000). Myeloid hormone analogues and methods for their preparation. *U.S. Patent No.* 4,220,000.

- Smith, T.S., Castelli, G., Yee, H., Maynard, J., Boxer, J.D. & Ribeiro, R.C.J. (1999). Selective myeloid hormone analogs. *U.S. Patent No.*

Non-Profit

This resume follows a functional layout, with skills emphasized and work history downplayed. Take a close look at Leticia's work history—she has held several short-term positions in varied fields and employers (legal service, association, union, and academic institutions). The functional layout is an effective way to emphasize competencies rather than the industries within which a candidate has worked. This style of resume is particularly good for people with little work experience, career changers, and those with gaps in their employment. Note: This style is not typically preferred in conservative arenas.

Leticia Roberts
Address
City, state, zip
Tel
e-mail

SKILLS AND EXPERIENCE

**Customer &
Member**

or Services

• Responded to in-coming calls for legal services agency, gave information about the organization, assessed whether caller could be served by the agency, and directed calls or Services made referrals when appropriate.

• Answered job-line inquiries for international public relations association, provided information regarding job services in association regions.

• Searched association's library files for communication and marketing information requested by members, or referred members to other association resources.

• Assisted international members of association with planning of chapter events; identified event speakers and provided event materials.

• Distributed materials for regional coordinators of study abroad organization, as well as for host families and student prospects. Assisted with processing of host and student applications, coordinated bulk mailings.

• Led small tutorial group for undergraduate political science course; facilitated discussions and advised students regarding term paper topics and writing.

**Computer &
Administrative**

• Proficiency with Microsoft Office (Word, Powerpoint and Excel) and the Internet.

• Maintained financial records for legal services agency and research and education department of international association. Responsible for donor tracking and recognition.

• Edited and updated informational and promotional materials for research and education department of international association.

• Researched text books and compiled annotated bibliography to compliment a syllabus for a college introductory course in comparative politics; generated ideas for term projects.

WORK HISTORY

12/01-present	Administrative Assistant; Child Care Law Center, San Francisco, CA
1/00-9/01	Members Assistant; International Association of Business Communicators, San Francisco, CA
11/99-9/00	Office Support Person; ASPECT Foundation, San Francisco, CA
11/98-4/99	Membership Services Officer; National Union of Teachers, United Kingdom.
1/98-5/98	Teaching Assistant; Political Science Department, Bryn Mawr College, PA.
Summer 1997	Coder; Medical Research Institute, Alcohol Research Group, Berkeley, CA.
Summer 1996	Intern; Buck Institute/College of Marin, Kentfield, CA.

EDUCATION

2003—Coursework in Asian and Latin American Art History, UC Berkeley Extension
B.A. in Political Science, Awarded Departmental Honors, Bryn Mawr College
Semester program emphasizing art history, Syracuse University in Florence, Italy

Career Change

Here's an example of a functional layout, with skills emphasized and work history downplayed. Bettina is an accomplished lawyer, but is changing careers to that of program manager/administrator. She targets three top skills she believes (based on careful research!) characterize program management. In addition to promoting her skills, this resume reflects the industry/fields with which she has expertise (disability rights and education).

BETTINA RAY MUELLER

45 Lakeshore Drive
Richmond, CA 94804
(510) 555-2773
bamueller@worldnet.att.net

QUALIFICATIONS

Organizational skills
- Coordinated day-to-day activity in 20 class action cases involving physical access to public accommodations
- Organized litigation project concerning physical and programmatic access in California schools
- Managed intake system for non-profit law firm receiving over 5000 calls a year
- Updated and maintained computer database of 100+ children's advocates

Communication skills
- Counseled and represented families in educational matters
- Resolved families' legal educational concerns through communication with school district personnel and counsel, social workers and probation officers
- Conducted workshops for community, professional, and parent groups
- Conducted interviews and deposition preparation with clients

Research and writing skills
- Drafted comments to Proposed Amendments to federal Individuals with Disabilities in Education Act
- Wrote federal and state memoranda of law, pleadings and discovery
- Analyzed and summarized voluminous document production
- Conducted legal research in substantive areas of education, disability, employment and civil rights law

EMPLOYMENT

Education Law Center, Intake Attorney, Philadelphia, PA	6/01-6/02
Disability Law Project, Attorney (Contract), Philadelphia, PA	3/01-5/01
Honeywell & Associates, Attorney, Philadelphia, PA	9/00-3/01
Disability Rights Advocates, Attorney, Oakland, CA	2/99-6/00

EDUCATION

Golden Gate University School of Law, Juris Doctor, San Francisco, CA, May 1999
Claremont Pitzer College, Bachelor of Arts, Anthroplogy/History, Claremont, CA, May 1995

Event Planner

This resume combines chronological with functional. This type of layout works well for an individual with a position of a lot of responsibility, and/or one with a multitude of skill areas. Kurt is an entrepreneur and has experience in every aspect of event planning and management; he organizes his achievements into broad skill areas within his position description. The resume is strong because it emphasizes quantifiable achievements as well as professional awards/recognition.

Kurt Williams, CMP
140 15th Avenue
San Francisco, California 94121
415-555-3434
kw@specialevents.com

SUMMARY

- Extensive experience in coordinating and organizing people, projects and events
- Highly skilled at developing and implementing program and marketing strategies
- Proven track record of completing multiple projects accurately and within budget
- Certified Meeting Professional

AWARDS

Top 25 Meeting and Event Planners in the Bay Area (Bay Area Business Express, 2002)
Top 15 Meeting and Event Planners in the Bay Area (Bay Area Business Express, 2001)

PROFESSIONAL EXPERIENCE

1998-present   **President** Special Events, Inc., San Francisco, CA

Event Planning
- Managed meetings with 90-2500 attendees with programs ranging from two days up to six days
- Developed, managed and administered program budgets from $60,000-$2.9 million
- Administered budget of $2.9 million, realizing $190,000 surplus
- Collaborated with Program Committee in implementing abstract review and acceptance procedure
- Coordinated speakers' scheduling, hotel arrangements, audio-visual requirements and expense reimbursements
- Managed all on-site operations

Trade Show
- Marketed and managed all logistics of exhibitor trade shows (management of drayage, decoration and security companies, exhibitor contracts and service manuals) with 12-90 vendors
- Inaugurated trade show for bi-annual conference, realizing 25% net profit on $12,500 in sales

Marketing
• Developed promotional programs and execution of collateral materials (logo, marketing announcements, preliminary program, call for abstracts, conference brochure, final program, show directory, conference mementos, convention signage) for conferences of various sizes
• Implemented and supervised direct mailing campaigns
• Wrote and edited marketing copy for product literature
• Analyzed campaign results to monitor effectiveness of marketing execution

Fundraising
• Developed sponsorship packages for bi-annual conference
• Implemented and supervised sponsorship mailing campaigns
• Cold-called targeted sponsor list, realizing $17,500 in donations
• Created first time silent and live auction, resulting in $14,000 income
• Developed cold-calling process for first time trade show, selling 14,000 square feet, generating $12,500 in revenue

Personnel Management
• Trained and directed registration team in handling of receipts, confirmations, cancellations
• Trained and managed paid staff and volunteer teams of up to 30 people

1997-1999   **Projects Coordinator** Golden State University, Fairfax, CA

Event Planning
• Coordinated and organized annual weeklong short course exceeding projected attendance by 30% resulting in 29% increase in net profits
• Managed visiting and distinguished lecturers, including travel, hotel and dinner arrangements

Kurt Williams, CMP page 2

OTHER EXPERIENCE

1996-1997 **Production Manager** Digital International, Fairfax, CA
1989-1995 **Journeyman Lithographer** Colorgraph, San Francisco, CA
1987-1989 **President** 5 Dimension Printing, San Francisco, CA

PROFESSIONAL AFFILIATIONS

1. Meeting Professionals International
2. Professional Convention Management Association (local chapter Board of Directors)

COMPUTER SKILLS

Macintosh platform: Microsoft Word, Excel, Access, PowerPoint, Outlook, Filemaker
Pro, PageMaker, QuarkXpress,
PC platform: Microsoft Word, Excel, Access, PowerPoint, Outlook, Filemaker Pro, Lotus

EDUCATION

1985 B.A., University of California, Irvine

Recipe for Success

What Happens Next?

- Contacting the Employer

- Before You Hit "Send"

- Following Up

- Thank-You Letters

- In Closing

Contacting the Employer

Congratulations! You now have the tools to put together killer cover letters and resumes that are carefully gauged to appeal to each of the employers you are targeting in your job search. The production of a winning application can be accomplished in three key steps:

1. Analyzing the position description and researching the employer

2. Assessing your own goals, skills, and achievements

3. Developing written materials that clearly articulate the match between you and the employer

Of course, the fourth step is actually contacting the prospective employer. This step probably involves the least overall effort, yet it's crucial in the process of winning interviews. Check out the following tips to ensure a smooth delivery aimed at evoking the best response from hiring managers and recruiters.

Before You Hit "Send"

Follow closely whatever instructions you have regarding sending your applications, especially if you're responding to an online job listing. This piece of advice may sound so basic, but a surprising number of candidates do not follow instructions and are automatically disqualified as a result. No one wants to hire a candidate that either can't follow instructions or doesn't pay attention.

Many if not most employers prefer to receive applications electronically, e-mailed directly or sent through the organization's human resource's website. Submitting your application this way does not mean taking a more informal approach in your writing.

Here are a few more basic tips for e-mailing your materials:

Subject line. Be sure the subject/header of the e-mail clearly states your reason for writing—for example: Application for Marketing Assistant Position.

Brief message. Include your "cover letter" as the text of your e-mail. You may want to make it a shortened version of a cover letter that you will send snail mail (or fax) as a follow up.

Testing 1 2 3. Include your resume as .doc or .txt attachment or in the text of your e-mail. Test the formatting by sending it to yourself or a friend before e-mailing it to a prospective employer.

What's in a name? Name your document after yourself, not "Resume_2002.doc" but "R.Jone02.doc." This way, the the recruiter or hiring manager can easily fish your document out of the sea of other resumes in his or her computer files.

What Next?

Following Up

What a relief! The writing, editing, and proofreading are finally over. The documents have been sent. Anticipation tingles up and down your spine as you daydream about the call you will get from the employer. Think you can relax? Think again. Support all that hard work by following through with an additional step. If you really, truly want the job, continue to show your interest *after* you have sent the application.

Place a phone call or send e-mail to confirm your materials were received and to reiterate your desire to learn more about the position. Don't become a nuisance, but do be persistent. After all, many employers look for people who take initiative and are good problem solvers.

Follow these basic guidelines for constructive follow-up, and you won't go wrong:

- **Be persistent but not pesky.** Two calls in one day are overkill; two calls in one week are probably fine.

- **Be prescriptive in your requests.** Ask specifically for what you want, whether it's to ensure the prospective employer has received your resume, to schedule an interview, or to have a casual chat on the phone.

- **Keep the ball in your court.** You'll probably feel more in control if you can plan the next steps rather than wait by the phone.

- **Make yourself easily available.** Provide a number where a message can be left at any time.

Employers say that at this early stage, there is a fine line between the interested candidate and the pesky one. But the hiring staff we interviewed unanimously said it couldn't hurt and could most definitely help your application if you take

What Next?

some time to follow up by contacting them in a respectful manner—a few calls or e-mails, and *that's it*.

If you need guidance on what to say, try adapting one of these scripts:

"This is Kelly Purcell. I sent you an application for the EMT position a few days ago and am following up to ensure you received my materials. Please let me know if you have any questions. If you are available to discuss my qualifications at greater length, I would like to schedule an interview. I can be reached today at 555-444-5555. On Thursday and Friday, it's best to call my cell phone, 555-657-6699. I'm looking forward to the chance to speak with you directly."

OR

"This is Merrill Morgan calling on Wednesday. I'm an MBA candidate from Fuqua with experience in the M&A group at UBS. At John Smith's request, I sent my resume to you on Monday. I would like to schedule an interview and will call you on Friday to discuss my qualifications."

In the latter script, the candidate leaves a brief message with some information on his background so the associate or recruiter will remember seeing the resume. He is specific about his plans to call back on Friday, which gives him an opportunity to check with John Smith.

If you've left three messages and all have been ignored, you may want to send your resume to someone else and try the process again. Many firms communicate primarily through voice mail, although you might have luck using e-mail or even leaving a good old-fashioned message with the receptionist. Tailor your approach to what you've learned about how that particular company communicates.

Thank-You Letters

Say that all your hard work, your customized cover letter and tailored resume, has led you to a meeting with an employer. Your research into the company and your own background helped you have a smooth and convincing interview. Or maybe the interview went pretty well, but there were a few points you wish you had made differently. (We've all been there!)

The thank-you letter is another tool you can use to add extra oomph to your candidacy. Short and sweet, this note shows gratitude for the time the employer has taken to review your qualifications, and it's an opportunity to demonstrate (again) that you are clearer than ever in your understanding of the fit between the position and your qualifications and goals. The thank-you letter has a bonus function, too: It gives you a final opportunity to address any weakness or clarify any misunderstanding that may have occurred in the interview process. The sample thank-you letter we've included mentions specifics of the meeting, shows appreciation, and reminds the employer of the candidate's strengths.

Sample E-Mailed Thank-You Letter

RE: Coordinator, Member Services – 2/26 Interview

February 27, 2003

Janet Lewis, Executive Director New York Global

Dear Janet,

I genuinely enjoyed meeting with you yesterday and learning more about New York Global and the clients you serve. I believe strongly that helping immigrants utilize their skills and training in a well-matched work environment is beneficial for both the individuals and the U.S. employers who hire them. I find the goals of your organization, in offering both direct services and advocacy on the issue of workforce diversity, to be admirable.

I was glad to be able to answer some of your questions regarding my background, approach to client services, and career goals. After our discussion, I continue to be eager to support the mission of New York Global and believe I could make a significant contribution as Coordinator of Member Services. In particular, my prior experience creating and delivering workforce diversity trainings and resources, along with my knowledge of local employers (developed through professional experience and through personal contacts as a native New Yorker) could serve your organization as you seek to build and strengthen client programming and outreach.

Please let me know if you have further questions, would like more information, or would like a list of my professional references. Feel free to contact me at your convenience via e-mail or telephone at (212) 555-1212. I look forward to hearing from you.

Sincerely,

Rachel Hertz, M.A.

rachelhertz@hotmail.com

What Next?

In Closing

The job search process doesn't have to feel like playing the lottery. With careful preparation, including researching employers and self-assessment, you can increase the odds that your application materials will get more than just a 30-second glance. No matter your background, experiences, or career goals, you can win interviews and job offers by creating thoughtful, direct, and informative cover letters and resumes.

For Your Reference

- Recommended Resources

- Books

- Surveys

- Author Bio

Recommended Resources

The resources that follow represent some of the best tools in developing job search materials. They correspond to suggestions we've made in this guide about preparation through research, and also provide access to more resume and cover letter information and samples. However, be aware that this is but a small sampling of the information that's available to help you effectively develop killer cover letters and resumes. So use the following as a jumping-off point in your research endeavors and feel free to explore the vast array of information that's out there on this topic.

Resumes and Letters

- Get resume feedback from a career or resume advisor. Most university career centers offer free resume consultations or workshops for students and for alumni at a nominal fee.

- Check out WetFeet's website for resume advice at www.wetfeet.com.

- Have a look at the Riley Guide, which comprises an extensive compilation of links to information on writing resumes and cover letters, as well as other useful job search information (www.rileyguide.com).

- Review content from Goinglobal, a WetFeet partner and a leading resource for guidance on international job searching, especially for country research and CV advice (www.wetfeet.com/research/countries.asp).

Researching Employers

- Use Google or another Internet search engine to find a company or organization's website (www.google.com).

- WetFeet.com Company Profiles give crucial insider information on top companies, including key indicators for success such as annual revenue, employee hiring numbers, and latest trends (www.wetfeet.com).

WetFeet®

- NewsDirectory.com or the *Business Times* (www. bizjournals.com) can help you in your search for current information on companies, organizations, and industry news.

Researching the Position

- The Occupational Outlook Handbook from the Bureau of Labor Statistics contains valuable information on occupational paths. Learn about qualifications, trends, and related occupations at http://www.bls.gov/oco/home.htm.

- WetFeet's Real People Profiles can give you a better understanding about the ins and outs of a variety of professions, and what it takes to succeed (www.wetfeet.com).

- Salary.com features searchable salary information by career categories and by location. Use this information to research and respond to salary expectation questions (www.salary.com).

- Job market and hiring trend information from NACE (National Association of Colleges and Employers) can keep you up to date on your job search (www.jobweb.com).

Industries and Fields

- The U.S. Department of Labor's America's Career InfoNet can give you a sense of the bigger picture on wages and employment trends (http://www.acinet.org/acinet/default.asp?tab=wagesandtrends).

- WetFeet Industry Profiles provide a fairly in-depth view of what it's like to work in various industries from accounting to venture capital (www.wetfeet.com).

- Search information on associations in almost every field or industry via online directories: the American Society of Association Executives (info.asaenet.org/gateway/onlineAssocslist.html) and the Internet Public Library's Database (www.ipl.org/div/aon).

- Associations often have useful industry and career path information on their websites, and contacting members can be a great way to network—one of the best sources of insider information for your job search.

Books

Your Rights in the Workplace

Barbara Kate Repa (Nolo Press)
This book does a good job of informing readers about their rights and
responsibilities as future employees.

Gallery of Best Cover Letters

David Noble (JIST Publishing)
This provides valuable cover letter samples across a wide spectrum of
industries, and with a wide variety of styles.

WetFeet Insider Guides

WetFeet's Insider Guides give you real insight into the industries and employers
that interest you most. Check out the additional titles available in the General
Career Help section on wetfeet.com to assist you with your job search. You'll
find guides that focus on everything from how to write entry-level resumes
(more samples!), ace your interviews, and negotiate a good salary.

Surveys

Here's more information about the two surveys cited in this book:

ResumeDoctor.com provides expert advice to job seekers, employers, and members of the media. ResumeDoctor.com is a subsidiary of Personal Department Inc. (PDI), Vermont's largest independently owned staffing agency. For more information, go to www.ResumeDoctor.com.

Since 1956, the **National Association of Colleges and Employers** (NACE) has been the leading source of information about the employment of college graduates. The *Job Outlook 2003* report forecasts the hiring intentions of employers and examines other issues related to the employment of new college graduates. NACE surveyed its employer members for the *Job Outlook 2003* report from mid-August through September 30, 2002; it is one of four NACE reports for the 2002 to 2003 academic year. Other reports for 2002 to 2003 include the *Job Outlook 2003 Fall Preview*, released in September 2002; the *Job Outlook 2003 Winter Update*, published in December 2002; and the *Job Outlook 2003 Spring Update*, published in April 2003. For more information, check out www.naceweb.com.

Author Bio

Rosanne Lurie, M.S., has been a career advisor in the Bay Area for more than six years, at public and private institutions, including University of California, San Francisco, and University of California, Berkeley. Her professional background includes delivery of career advice through individual counseling and workshops, as well as developing and managing online and print resources for career center websites and libraries. In addition to orienting undergrads to career planning, she has worked with graduate students and alumni to develop their job searching skills for academic, clinical, and industry positions. A San Francisco native, she attended Haverford College near Philadelphia and earned a master's degree in counseling from San Francisco State University. As a career advisor, she enjoys helping her clients choose their career direction and pursue their life goals.

WetFeet's Insider Guide Series

Ace Your Case! The WetFeet Insider Guide to Consulting Interviews
Ace Your Case II: Fifteen More Consulting Cases
Ace Your Case III: Practice Makes Perfect
Ace Your Case IV: The Latest and Greatest
Ace Your Interview! The WetFeet Insider Guide to Interviewing
Beat the Street: The WetFeet Insider Guide to Investment Banking Interviews
Getting Your Ideal Internship
Get Your Foot in the Door! Landing the Job Interview
Job Hunting A to Z: The WetFeet Insider Guide to Landing the Job You Want
Killer Consulting Resumes!
Killer Cover Letters and Resumes!
Killer Investment Banking Resumes!
Negotiating Your Salary and Perks
Networking Works! The WetFeet Insider Guide to Networking

Career and Industry Guides

Accounting
Advertising and Public Relations
Asset Management and Retail Brokerage
Biotech and Pharmaceuticals
Brand Management
Computer Software and Hardware
Consulting for Ph.D.s, Lawyers, and Doctors
Entertainment and Sports
Health Care
Human Resources
Industries and Careers for MBAs
Industries and Careers for Undergrads
Information Technology
Investment Banking
Management Consulting

Marketing and Market Research

Non-Profits and Government Agencies

Oil and Gas

Real Estate

Top 20 Biotechnology and Pharmaceutical Firms

Top 25 Consulting Firms

Top 25 Financial Services Firms

Top 20 Law Firms

Venture Capital

Company Guides

Accenture

Bain & Company

Bear Stearns

Booz Allen Hamilton

The Boston Consulting Group

Cap Gemini Ernst & Young

Citigroup

Credit Suisse First Boston

Deloitte Consulting

Goldman Sachs

IBM Business Consulting Services

JPMorgan Chase

Lehman Brothers

McKinsey & Company

Merrill Lynch

Monitor Group

Morgan Stanley